oh!
my SPEAKING 5

CEDU BOOK

UNIT COMPONENTS

• KEY PATTERNS

Key words and key patterns are presented in context.
Students can role-play the conversation used in the cartoon.

• VOCABULARY

Vocabulary words can be used immediately through activities related to pattern sentences.

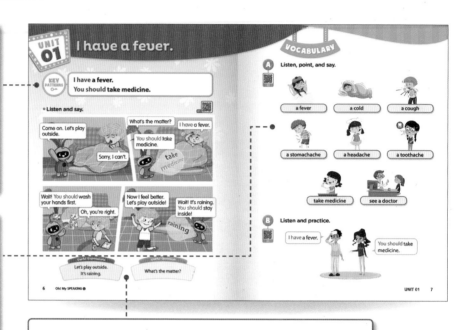

• USEFUL EXPRESSIONS & QUESTIONS

A variety of particularly useful expressions from the dialogues in the cartoons allow students to develop their speaking skills.

• KEY PATTERN PRACTICE

Repeating sentences with key patterns helps students to naturally remember what they have learned.

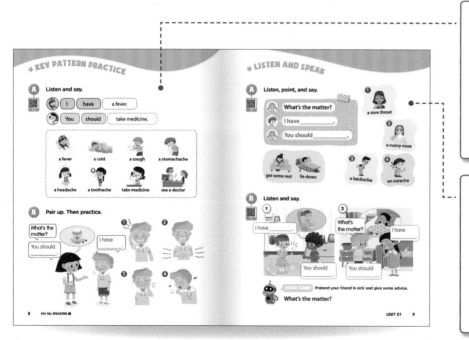

• LISTEN AND SPEAK

Substituting words in key patterns in a combined listening and speaking activity assists students to build their speaking fluency.

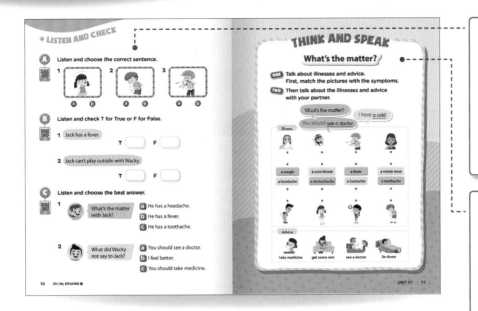

• LISTEN AND CHECK

Listening practice gets students to relate the key sentences to the pictures and to learn how to use the right sentences in the conversation.

• THINK AND SPEAK

A fun and educational communication game gets students to practice key sentences repeatedly.

REVIEW TEST

Word reviews and a variety of speaking and listening activities help students recall and further practice key words and key patterns from previous units.

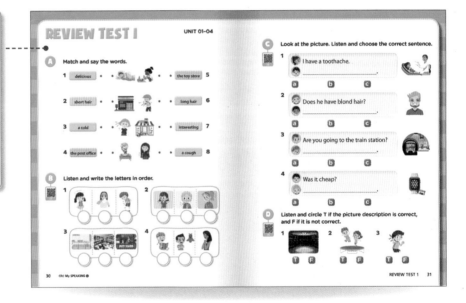

WORKBOOK

Various writing, listening, and speaking exercises allow students to review key words and key patterns learned in the Student Book.

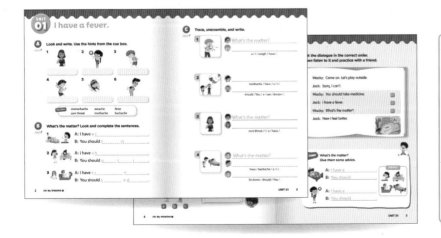

CONTENTS

UNIT 01

I have a fever.

I have a fever.
You should take medicine.

● **Listen and say.**

Come on. Let's play outside.

Sorry, I can't.

What's the matter?

I have a fever.

You should take medicine.

take medicine

Wait! You should wash your hands first.

Oh, you're right.

Now I feel better. Let's play outside!

Wait! It's raining. You should stay inside!

raining

Useful Expressions

Let's play outside.
It's raining.

Useful Question

What's the matter?

VOCABULARY

A Listen, point, and say.

(a fever)

(a cold)

(a cough)

(a stomachache)

(a headache)

(a toothache)

(take medicine)

(see a doctor)

B Listen and practice.

I have a fever.

You should take medicine.

★ KEY PATTERN PRACTICE

 A **Listen and say.**

I have a fever.

You should take medicine.

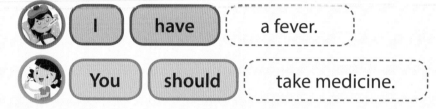

a fever   a cold   a cough   a stomachache

a headache   a toothache   take medicine   see a doctor

B **Pair up. Then practice.**

What's the matter?

You should _____.

I have _____.

❶ ❷ ❸ ❹

★ LISTEN AND SPEAK

A Listen, point, and say.

What's the matter?

I have _____.

You should _____.

① a sore throat

② a runny nose

get some rest   lie down

③ a backache   ④ an earache

B Listen and say.

① I have _____.

You should _____.

② What's the matter?

I have _____.

You should _____.

YOUR TURN! Pretend your friend is sick and give some advice.

What's the matter?

A Listen and choose the correct sentence.

1
a   b

2
a   b

3
a   b

B Listen and check T for True or F for False.

1 Jack has a fever.

T ☐   F ☐

2 Jack can't play outside with Wacky.

T ☐   F ☐

C Listen and choose the best answer.

1 What's the matter with Jack?

a He has a headache.

b He has a fever.

c He has a toothache.

2 What did Wacky not say to Jack?

a You should see a doctor.

b I feel better.

c You should take medicine.

THINK AND SPEAK

What's the matter?

ONE Talk about illnesses and advice.
First, match the pictures with the symptoms.

TWO Then talk about the illnesses and advice
with your partner.

What's the matter?

I have a cold.

You should see a doctor.

Illness

| a cough | a sore throat | a fever | a runny nose |
| a headache | a stomachache | a backache | a toothache |

Advice

take medicine   get some rest   see a doctor   lie down

He has long hair.

KEY PATTERNS

He has **long hair.** / He doesn't have **a beard.**
He wears **big glasses.** / He doesn't wear **a tie.**

Listen and say.

Does he have long hair?

Yes. He has long hair.

Does he have a beard?

No. He doesn't have a beard.

Does he wear glasses?

Yes. He wears big glasses.

Does he wear a tie?

No. He doesn't wear a tie. There he is!

Hi, Uncle Joe!

Useful Expression

There he is!

Useful Questions

Does he have long hair?
Does he wear glasses?

VOCABULARY

A Listen, point, and say.

long hair

short hair

straight hair

curly hair

a beard

a tie

a necklace

a headband

B Listen and practice.

He has **long hair.**
He wears **a tie.**

She doesn't have **short hair.**
She doesn't wear **a tie.**

★ KEY PATTERN PRACTICE

A Listen and say.

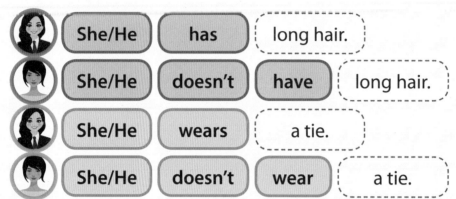

She/He	has	long hair.
She/He	doesn't	have	long hair.
She/He	wears	a tie.
She/He	doesn't	wear	a tie.

long hair   short hair   straight hair   curly hair

a beard   a tie   a necklace   a headband

B Pair up. Then practice.

He has _____ .

He wears _____ .

Does she have straight hair?

No. She doesn't have _____ .
She has _____ .

Does she wear a tie?

No. She doesn't wear _____ .
She wears _____ .

14   Oh! My SPEAKING ⑤

★ LISTEN AND SPEAK

 Listen, point, and say.

He/She has _____ .

He/She wears _____ .

He/She doesn't have _____ .

He/She doesn't wear _____ .

① blond hair

② a ponytail

a ring

a bracelet

③ pigtails

④ a mustache

B Listen and say.

1

Does he have blond hair?

Yes. He has _____ , and he wears _____ .

2

There's Kate.
She has _____ .

Does she wear a bracelet?

No. She doesn't wear _____ .

YOUR TURN! Ask and answer questions about your friends' appearance.

Does she have long hair?

★ LISTEN AND CHECK

A Listen and choose the correct sentence.

1  ⓐ ⓑ

2  ⓐ ⓑ

3  ⓐ ⓑ

B Listen and number.

C Listen and choose the correct sentence for the blank.

1 Does he have a mustache?

ⓐ ⓑ ⓒ _____

2 Does she wear a headband?

ⓐ ⓑ ⓒ _____

THINK AND SPEAK

Guess Who?

ONE Pair up.

TWO Take turns describing one person from the picture below.

THREE While you describe the person, your friend should guess who it is.

Guess who?
He wears glasses.
He doesn't wear sneakers.

Does he have a beard?

Yes. He has a beard.

It's Mr. Adams!

Mr. Adams   Tom   Amy   Min   Michael   Miss James

UNIT 03
I'm going to the airport.

I'm going to the airport.
I'm not going to the airport.

• **Listen and say.**

Where are you going?

I'm going to the airport. I'm going to Switzerland.

I'm going to the science fair in Switzerland.

Wow, lucky!

Are you going to the airport, too?

No. I'm not going to the airport.

I'm going to the train station. I'm going to my grandmother's house in Busan.

Lucky!

Useful Expression

Lucky!

Useful Questions

Where are you going?
Are you going to the airport?

VOCABULARY

A Listen, point, and say.

the airport

the train station

the subway station

the science fair

the post office

the department store

the zoo

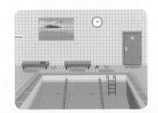
the swimming pool

the clothing store

B Listen and practice.

I'm going to the airport.

I'm not going to the airport. I'm going to the train station.

✴ KEY PATTERN PRACTICE

A Listen and say.

Are you going to the airport?

 Yes. **I'm** **going to** the airport.

 No. **I'm** **not** **going to** the airport.

 the airport

 the train station

 the subway station

 the science fair

 the post office

 the department store

 the zoo

 the swimming pool

 the clothing store

B Pair up. Then practice.

Are you going to the train station?

Where are you going?

No. I'm not going to the train station. I'm going to _____.

I'm going to _____.

★ LISTEN AND SPEAK

A Listen, point, and say.

Are you going to _____?

Yes. I'm going to _____.

No. I'm not going to _____.

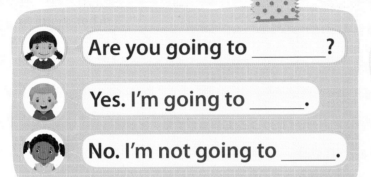

1  the concert hall

2 the pet shop

3  the toy store

4  the aquarium

5  the supermarket

6  the sports center

B Listen and say.

1

Where are you going?

I'm going to _____.

2

Are you going to _____?

No. I'm not going to _____. I'm going to _____.

 **YOUR TURN!** Talk about the place you're going to.

Where are you going?

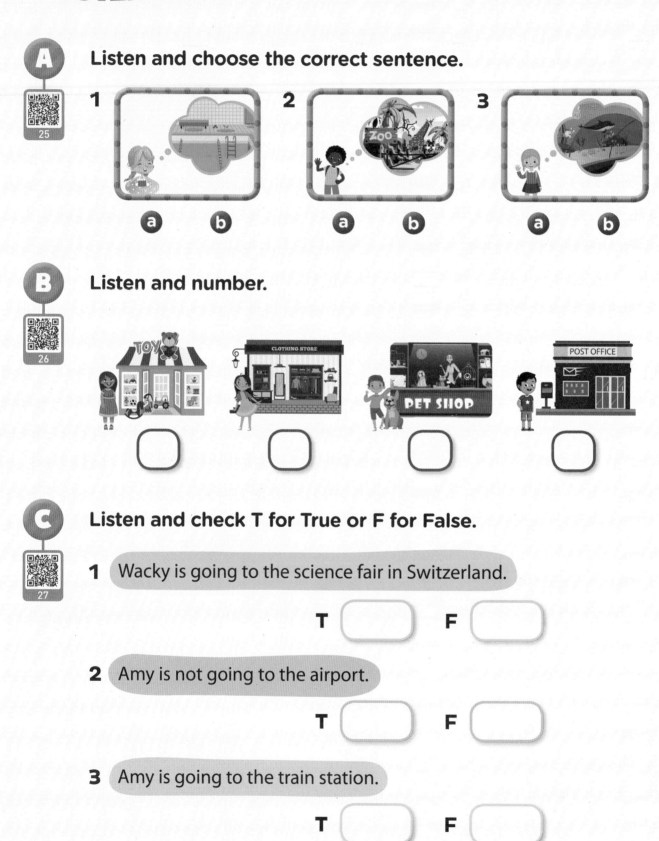

A Listen and choose the correct sentence.

1 ⓐ ⓑ

2 ⓐ ⓑ

3 ⓐ ⓑ

B Listen and number.

TOY   CLOTHING STORE   PET SHOP   POST OFFICE

C Listen and check T for True or F for False.

1 Wacky is going to the science fair in Switzerland.

T ⬜   F ⬜

2 Amy is not going to the airport.

T ⬜   F ⬜

3 Amy is going to the train station.

T ⬜   F ⬜

THINK AND SPEAK

Where are you going?

ONE Pair up.

TWO Roll the die and ask "Where are you going?" for 1, 3, or 5; or "Are you going to the supermarket?" for 2, 4, or 6.

THREE Your friend rolls the die and answers according to the number.

Where are you going?

I'm going to the train station.

   Student 1 Student 2

Are you going to the supermarket?

No. I'm not going to the supermarket. I'm going to the post office.

   Student 1 Student 2

START	The Science Fair	The Train Station	Jump ahead four	The Post Office
				Anywhere you want
Jump ahead one	The Zoo	The Concert Hall	The Department Store	Go back two
The Aquarium				
The Pet Shop	Anywhere you want	The Toy Store	The Swimming Pool	FINISH

It was funny.

KEY PATTERNS

It was funny.
It wasn't funny.

wasn't = was not

• Listen and say.

How was the movie?

I loved it! It was a comedy.

It was funny and exciting!

It wasn't funny. It was boring.

Was it too long?

Yes. It was too long.

But the popcorn was delicious.

Oh my!

Useful Expressions

I loved it!
Oh my!

Useful Questions

How was the movie?
Was it too long?

VOCABULARY

A Listen, point, and say.

funny   boring   exciting

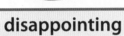

disappointing   great   delicious

cheap   expensive

B Listen and practice.

It was funny.   It wasn't funny.

★ KEY PATTERN PRACTICE

Was it funny?

Yes. **It** **was** funny.

No. **It** **wasn't** funny.

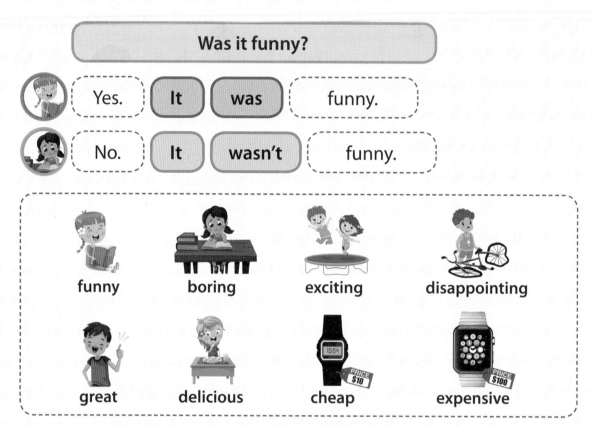

funny	boring	exciting	disappointing
great	delicious	cheap	expensive

B Pair up. Then practice.

How was the movie?

It was _____.

Was it expensive?

No. It wasn't expensive.
It was _____.

★ LISTEN AND SPEAK

A Listen, point, and say.

Was it _____?

Yes. It was _____.

No. It wasn't _____.

1 interesting

2 shocking

3 difficult

4 amazing

5 touching

6 scary

B Listen and say.

1

How was the movie?

It was _____.

2

How was the movie?
Was it interesting?

No. It wasn't _____.
It was _____.

YOUR TURN! Ask and answer how you felt about it.

How was the movie?

★ LISTEN AND CHECK

A Listen and choose the correct sentence.

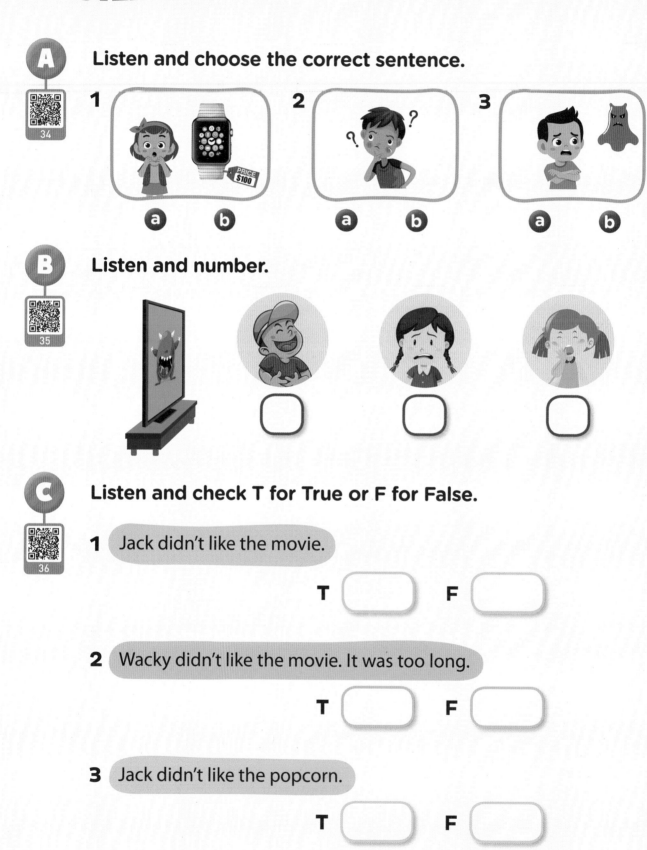

1 a b

2 a b

3 a b

B Listen and number.

C Listen and check T for True or F for False.

1 Jack didn't like the movie.

T ☐ F ☐

2 Wacky didn't like the movie. It was too long.

T ☐ F ☐

3 Jack didn't like the popcorn.

T ☐ F ☐

THINK AND SPEAK

How was...?

ONE Look at each picture below and write the word that best describes how you felt about it.

TWO Pair up and say.

funny	boring	exciting	interesting	great
shocking	disappointing	difficult	amazing	scary

How was the library?

It was boring.

the library

boring

the soccer game

the horror movie

the class

the test

the trip

A Match and say the words.

1 delicious •

• the toy store 5

2 short hair •

• long hair 6

3 a cold •

• interesting 7

4 the post office •

• a cough 8

B Listen and write the letters in order.

1

2

3

4

C Look at the picture. Listen and choose the correct sentence.

1

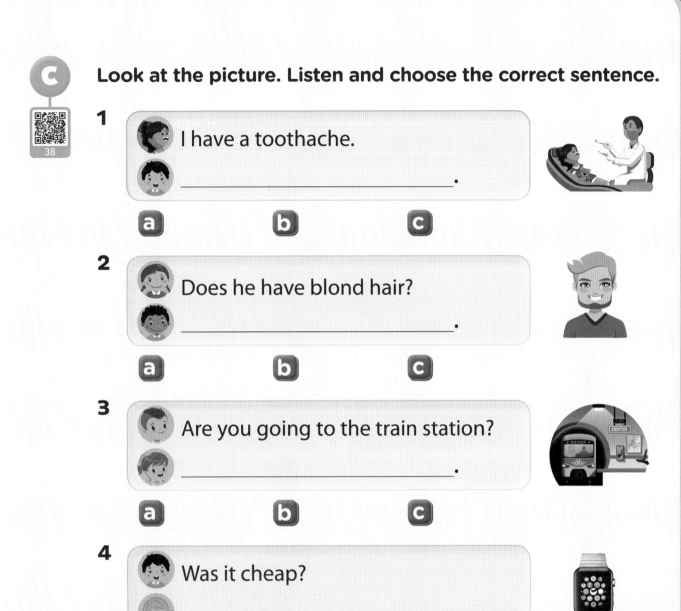

I have a toothache.

_____.

a   b   c

2

Does he have blond hair?

_____.

a   b   c

3

Are you going to the train station?

_____.

a   b   c

4

Was it cheap?

_____.

a   b   c

D Listen and circle T if the picture description is correct, and F if it is not correct.

1 T   F   **2** T   F   **3** T   F

REVIEW TEST I

E **Describe your friend.**

STEP I Choose and write the correct sentences for each blank.

He doesn't have a beard

He doesn't wear glasses

He wears a tie

He has long hair

Can you find Joe?

Yes. _____.

No. _____.

No. _____.
_____.

Yes, I can.
Does he have long hair?

Does he have a beard?

Does he wear glasses?

Oh! There he is!

STEP 2 Check the boxes. Then draw the friend who you are going to introduce.

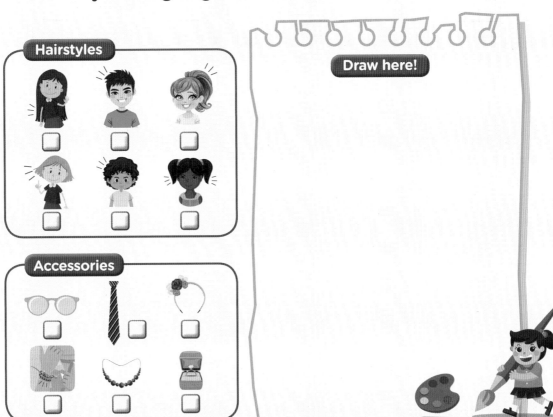

Hairstyles

Draw here!

Accessories

STEP 3 What does your friend look like? Write and talk about him or her with your friends.

Here's my friend _____.
(name)

He/She has _____.

He/She doesn't have _____.

He/She wears _____.

He/She doesn't wear _____.

UNIT 05

I'm interested in adventure stories.

I'm interested in adventure stories.
I'm not interested in horror stories.

I'm = I am

Listen and say.

40

What kind of books do you like?

BOOKSTORE

I'm interested in adventure stories.

Are you interested in sci-fi stories?

BOOKSTORE

Yes. I'm interested in sci-fi stories.

How about horror stories?

No. I'm not interested in horror stories.

You really enjoy reading books!

BOOKSTORE

Yes, we do.

Useful Expression

You really enjoy reading books!

Useful Questions

What kind of books do you like?
How about horror stories?

VOCABULARY

A Listen, point, and say.

adventure stories

sci-fi stories

horror stories

comic books

action movies

comedies

classical music

hip-hop

B Listen and practice.

I'm interested in adventure stories.

I'm not interested in adventure stories.

★ KEY PATTERN PRACTICE

A **Listen and say.**

Are you interested in adventure stories?

Yes. **I'm** **interested in** adventure stories.

No. **I'm** **not** **interested in** adventure stories.

adventure stories

sci-fi stories

horror stories

comic books

action movies

comedies

classical music

hip-hop

B **Pair up. Then practice.**

What kind of books do you like?

1 Sci-fi Stories **2** Comic Books

I'm interested in _____.

Are you interested in action movies?

No. I'm not interested in action movies. I'm interested in _____.

★ LISTEN AND SPEAK

A Listen, point, and say.

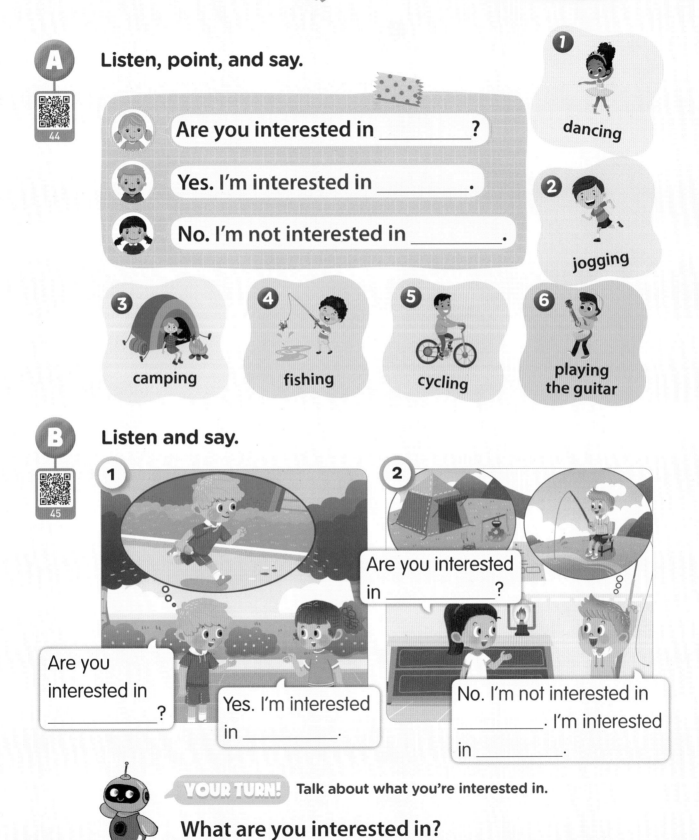

Are you interested in _____?

Yes. I'm interested in _____.

No. I'm not interested in _____.

1 dancing

2 jogging

3 camping

4 fishing

5 cycling

6 playing the guitar

B Listen and say.

1

Are you interested in _____?

Yes. I'm interested in _____.

2

Are you interested in _____?

No. I'm not interested in _____. I'm interested in _____.

YOUR TURN! Talk about what you're interested in.

What are you interested in?

★ LISTEN AND CHECK

A Listen and choose the correct sentence.

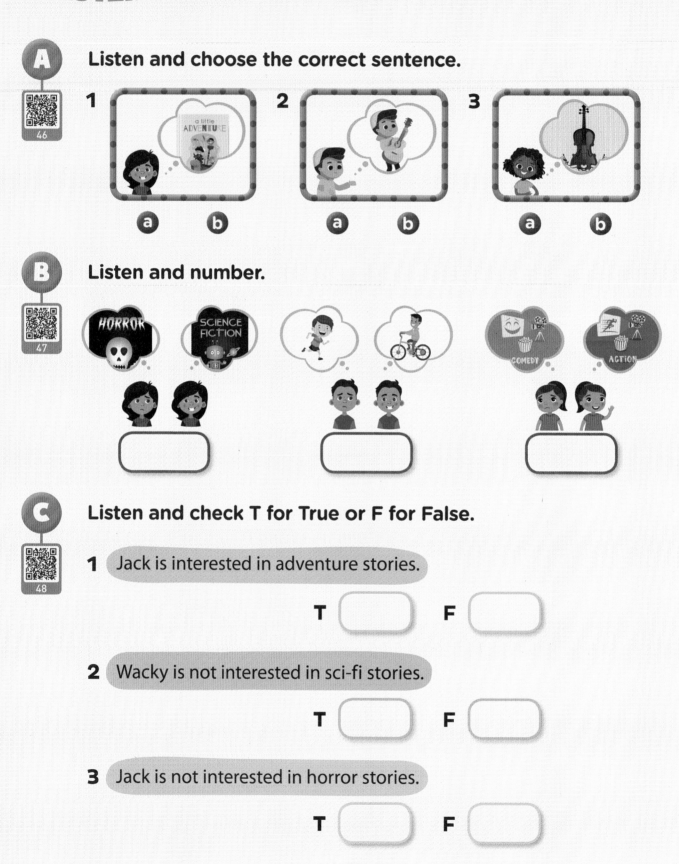

1

a   b

2

a   b

3

a   b

B Listen and number.

HORROR   SCIENCE FICTION

COMEDY   ACTION

C Listen and check T for True or F for False.

1 Jack is interested in adventure stories.

T   F

2 Wacky is not interested in sci-fi stories.

T   F

3 Jack is not interested in horror stories.

T   F

THINK AND SPEAK

I'm interested in...

ONE Gather three in one group. Each one chooses their interests.

TWO One says the first sentence.

THREE Then the others repeat the previous sentence, adding another item of their own to the sentence.

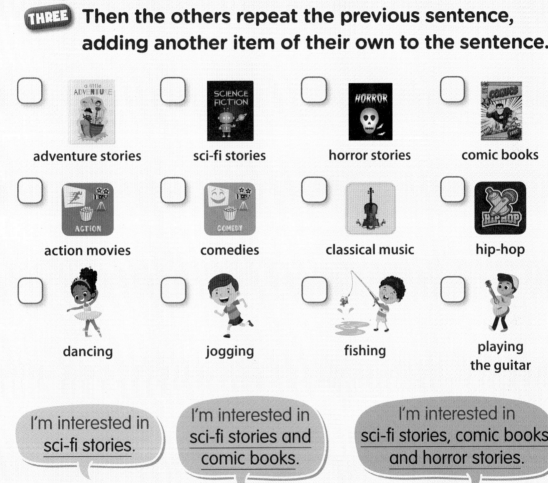

adventure stories	sci-fi stories	horror stories	comic books
action movies	comedies	classical music	hip-hop
dancing	jogging	fishing	playing the guitar

I'm interested in sci-fi stories.

I'm interested in sci-fi stories and comic books.

I'm interested in sci-fi stories, comic books, and horror stories.

Student 1

Student 2

Student 3

UNIT 06

I want to be a scientist.

KEY PATTERNS

I want to be a scientist.

I don't want to be a scientist.

don't = do not

• Listen and say.

49

What do you want to be?

I like science, so...

I want to be a scientist... like you.

Awesome!

Amy, do you want to be a scientist, too?

No. I don't want to be a scientist. I want to be a teacher.

Jack, sit down. Open your book.

No. I don't want to study now.

Useful Expressions

Like you.

Open your book.

Useful Questions

What do you want to be?

Do you want to be a scientist?

VOCABULARY

A Listen, point, and say.

a dancer

a fashion designer

a lawyer

a pianist

a pilot

a reporter

an actor

an artist

B Listen and practice.

I want to be a dancer.

I don't want to be a dancer. I want to be a fashion designer.

★ KEY PATTERN PRACTICE

 A Listen and say.

> **Do you want to be a dancer?**

Yes. **I** **want** **to be** a dancer.

No. **I** **don't** **want** **to be** a dancer.

 a dancer

 a fashion designer

 a lawyer

 a pianist

 a pilot

 a reporter

 an actor

 an artist

B Pair up. Then practice.

What do you want to be?

I want to be _____.

Do you want to be a dancer?

No. I don't want to be a dancer. I want to be _____.

★ LISTEN AND SPEAK

A Listen, point, and say.

1 a firefighter

Do you want to be _____?

Yes. I want to be _____.

2 a singer

No. I don't want to be _____.

3 a photographer

4 a movie director

5 an astronaut

6 an architect

B Speak about yourself.

What do you want to be?

1 I want to be _____.

2 I want to be _____.

3 I want to be _____.

YOUR TURN! Talk about your dream job.

What do you want to be?

★ LISTEN AND CHECK

A Listen and choose the correct sentence.

1
a   b

2
a   b

3
a   b

B Listen and number.

C Listen and check T for True or F for False.

1 Jack likes science.

T   F

2 Jack doesn't want to be a scientist.

T   F

3 Amy wants to be a scientist and a teacher.

T   F

THINK AND SPEAK

My Dream Job

ONE Pair up. Choose one dream job card.

TWO Mime the content of the card to your friend.
Your friend should guess what job you are miming.
Then take turns.

What do you want to be?
Do you want to be
a scientist?

No. I don't want to be
a scientist.

Do you want to be a pilot?

Yes. I want to be a pilot.

I'm going to make a boat.

KEY PATTERNS

I'm going to make a boat.
I'm not going to make a boat.

I'm = I am

• **Listen and say.**

57

What are you going to do with the chopsticks?

I'm going to make something.

I'm going to make a boat. I'm going to float it on the water.

Wow!

Are you going to make a boat, too?

No. I'm not going to make a boat. I'm going to make a kite.

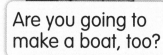

I'm going to fly it by the pond.

Good idea! Let's go together.

Useful Expression

Let's go together.

Useful Questions

What are you going to do?
Are you going to make a boat?

VOCABULARY

A Listen, point, and say.

make a boat

make a kite

float a boat

fly an airplane

blow bubbles

play with clay

take a trip

go hiking

B Listen and practice.

I'm going to make a boat.

I'm not going to make a boat. I'm going to make a kite.

★ KEY PATTERN PRACTICE

A Listen and say.

Are you going to make a boat?

Yes. | I'm | going to | make a boat.

No. | I'm | not | going to | make a boat.

make a boat | make a kite | float a boat | fly an airplane

blow bubbles | play with clay | take a trip | go hiking

B Pair up. Then practice.

1 **2**

What are you going to do?

I'm going to _____.

3 **4**

Are you going to play with clay?

No. I'm not going to play with clay. I'm going to _____.

★ LISTEN AND SPEAK

A Listen, point, and say.

Are you going to _____?

Yes. I'm going to _____.

No. I'm not going to _____.

① blow up a balloon

② climb a rock wall

③ make origami

④ play with friends

⑤ take a walk

⑥ take a nap

B Listen and say.

1

What are you going to do? Are you going to _____?

Yes. I'm going to _____.

2

Are you going to _____?

No. I'm not going to _____. I'm going to _____.

YOUR TURN! Talk about what you're going to do in your free time.

What are you going to do?

A Listen and choose the correct sentence.

1   a   b   **2**   a   b   **3**   a   b

B Listen and number.

C Listen and check T for True or F for False.

1 Jack is going to make a boat.

T   F

2 Wacky is going to make a kite.

T   F

3 Wacky is going to fly a kite by the pond.

T   F

THINK AND SPEAK

Weekend Plan

ONE Fill in the blanks below with what you are going to do this weekend.

TWO Pair up. Ask and answer.

> What are you going to do on <u>Saturday morning</u>?

> I'm going to <u>take a trip</u>.

	Me	Partner
Saturday morning		
Saturday afternoon		
Sunday morning		
Sunday afternoon		

UNIT 08

I'll go to the library.

I'll go to the library.
I won't go to the library.

I'll = I will
won't = will not

• **Listen and say.**

66

I'll go to the library and borrow some books.

I'll go with you.

I'll do my homework there.

Okay. Wacky, will you come with us?

No. I won't go to the library. I'll just stay home.

What will you do?

I'll play a computer game, but I won't play too much.

Okay. See you later.

Useful Expression

See you later.

Useful Questions

Will you come with us?
What will you do?

VOCABULARY

A Listen, point, and say.

go to the library

stay home

borrow some books

go on a picnic

visit one's uncle's house

eat out

read comic books

get a haircut

B Listen and practice.

I'll go to the library.

I won't go to the library. I'll stay home.

★ KEY PATTERN PRACTICE

A Listen and say.

Will you go to the library?

| Yes. | **I'll** | go | to the library. |

*I'll = I will

| No. | **I** | **won't** | go | to the library. |

*won't = will not

 go to
the library

 stay home

 borrow
some books

 go on a picnic

 visit one's
uncle's house

 eat out

 read
comic books

 get a haircut

B Pair up. Then practice.

1 2 3 4

What will you do?

I'll _____.

Will you stay home?

No. I won't stay home. I'll _____.

★ LISTEN AND SPEAK

A Listen, point, and say.

Will you _____ ?

Yes. I'll _____ .

No. I won't _____ .

1 have a birthday party

2 have a barbecue

3 go to the movies

4 go to the concert

5 go shopping

6 stay up late

B Speak about yourself.

What will you do?

1 I will _____ .

2 I will _____ .

3 I will _____ .

YOUR TURN! Ask and answer what you'll do this weekend.

What will you do?

★ LISTEN AND CHECK

A Listen and choose the correct sentence.

1 **2** **3**

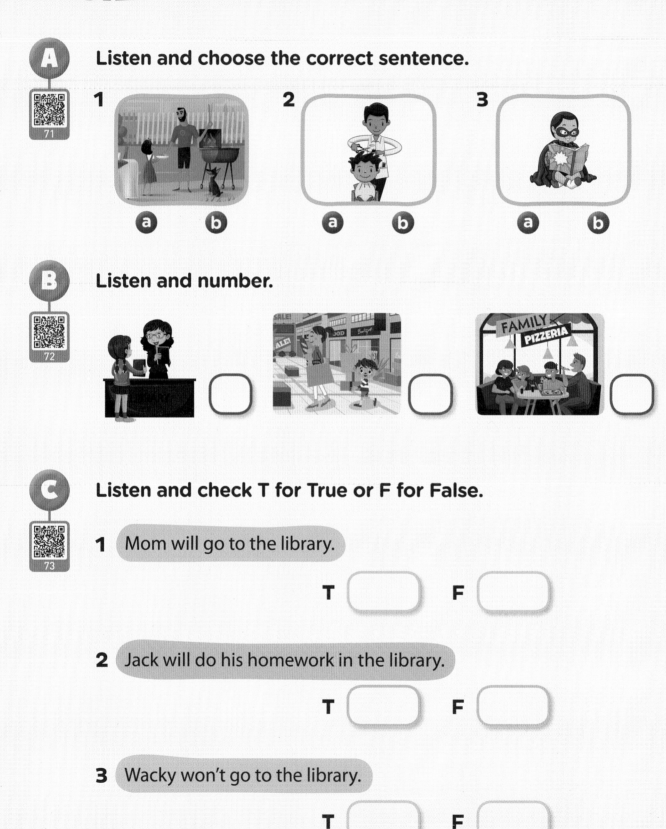

a   b   a   b   a   b

B Listen and number.

C Listen and check T for True or F for False.

1 Mom will go to the library.

T   F

2 Jack will do his homework in the library.

T   F

3 Wacky won't go to the library.

T   F

THINK AND SPEAK

My Weekly Planner

ONE Fill in the blanks in the chart with your own plans.

TWO Compare it with your friend's plan chart.

THREE Talk about your plans together as suggested below.

What will you do on Monday?

I'll go to the library (and read some books).

Will you go on a picnic on Tuesday?

No. I won't go on a picnic on Tuesday. (It'll rain.)

	Activities
Mon	
Tues	
Wed	
Thurs	
Fri	
Sat	
Sun	

Yours

	Activities
Mon	
Tues	
Wed	
Thurs	
Fri	
Sat	
Sun	

Your Friend's

REVIEW TEST 2

A Match and say the words.

1 sci-fi stories •

2 a movie director •

3 horror stories •

4 a pianist •

5 blow bubbles

6 get a haircut

7 make origami

8 eat out

B Listen and write the letters in order.

1

2

3

4

Look at the picture. Listen and choose the correct sentence.

1

Are you interested in playing the guitar?

_____.

a　　　　**b**　　　　**c**

2

What do you want to be?

_____.

a　　　　**b**　　　　**c**

3

Are you going to climb a rock wall?

_____.

a　　　　**b**　　　　**c**

4

What will you do?
Will you go on a picnic?

_____.

a　　　　**b**　　　　**c**

D **Listen and circle T if the picture description is correct, and F if it is not correct.**

1　**T**　**F**　　**2**　**T**　**F**　　**3**　**T**　**F**

E Talk about yourself.

STEP 1 Choose and write the correct words for each blank.

I'm interested in hip-hop

I want to be a singer

I'm ten

I'm Amy

Nice to meet you. I'm Tom.

Nice to meet you, too. _____.

How old are you?

_____ years old.

What are you interested in? Are you interested in hip-hop?

Yes. _____.

What do you want to be?

I like music, so _____.

Awesome!

STEP 2 Draw circles around your interests and your dream jobs.

Interests

Dream Jobs

STEP 3 What do you want to be?
Write and talk about it with your friends.

I'm _____.
(name)

I'm _____.
(age)

I'm interested in _____.

I like _____,

so I want to be _____.
(dream job)

SCOPE & SEQUENCE

UNIT 01   I have a fever.

Key Patterns	Vocabulary	Useful Expressions	Goals
I have a fever. You should take medicine.	a fever / a cold / a cough / a stomachache / a headache / a toothache / take medicine / see a doctor / a sore throat / a runny nose / a backache / an earache / get some rest / lie down	Let's play outside. It's raining. **Useful Question** What's the matter?	• Talking about illnesses • Advising ● **Theme** Health

UNIT 02   He has long hair.

Key Patterns	Vocabulary	Useful Expression	Goals
He has long hair. He doesn't have a beard. He wears big glasses. He doesn't wear a tie.	long hair / short hair / straight hair / curly hair / a beard / a tie / a necklace / a headband / blond hair / a ponytail / pigtails / a mustache / a ring / a bracelet	There he is! **Useful Questions** Does he have long hair? Does he wear glasses?	• Describing a third person's appearances and accessories • Making affirmative/negative statements ● **Theme** Describing people

UNIT 03   I'm going to the airport.

Key Patterns	Vocabulary	Useful Expression	Goals
I'm going to the airport. I'm not going to the airport.	the airport / the train station / the subway station / the science fair / the post office / the department store / the zoo / the swimming pool / the clothing store / the concert hall / the pet shop / the toy store / the aquarium / the supermarket / the sports center	Lucky! **Useful Questions** Where are you going? Are you going to the airport?	• Talking about destinations • Using the present continuous tense to express intention • Making affirmative/negative statements ● **Theme** Destinations

UNIT 04   It was funny.

Key Patterns	Vocabulary	Useful Expressions	Goals
It was funny. It wasn't funny.	funny / boring / exciting / disappointing / great / delicious / cheap / expensive / interesting / shocking / difficult / amazing / touching / scary	I loved it! Oh my! **Useful Questions** How was the movie? Was it too long?	• Talking about feelings • Using the verb "be" in the past tense • Making affirmative/negative statements ● **Theme** Feelings

REVIEW TEST 1   **UNIT 01-04**

UNIT 05   I'm interested in adventure stories.

Key Patterns	Vocabulary	Useful Expression	Goals
I'm interested in adventure stories. I'm not interested in horror stories.	adventure stories / sci-fi stories / horror stories / comic books / action movies / comedies / classical music / hip-hop / dancing / jogging / camping / fishing / cycling / playing the guitar	You really enjoy reading books! **Useful Questions** What kind of books do you like? How about horror stories?	• Talking about interests • Making affirmative/negative statements ● **Theme** Hobbies

UNIT 06   I want to be a scientist.

Key Patterns	Vocabulary	Useful Expressions	Goals
I want to be a scientist. I don't want to be a scientist.	a dancer / a fashion designer / a lawyer / a pianist / a pilot / a reporter / an actor / an artist / a firefighter / a singer / a photographer / a movie director / an astronaut / an architect	Like you. Open your book. **Useful Questions** What do you want to be? Do you want to be a scientist?	• Talking about future dreams • Making affirmative/negative statements ● **Theme** Future dreams

UNIT 07   I'm going to make a boat.

Key Patterns	Vocabulary	Useful Expression	Goals
I'm going to make a boat. I'm not going to make a boat.	make a boat / make a kite / float a boat / fly an airplane / blow bubbles / play with clay / take a trip / go hiking / blow up a balloon / climb a rock wall / make origami / play with friends / take a walk / take a nap	Let's go together. **Useful Questions** What are you going to do? Are you going to make a boat?	• Talking about plans with "be going to" • Making affirmative/negative statements ● **Theme** Free time / Plans

UNIT 08   I'll go to the library.

Key Patterns	Vocabulary	Useful Expression	Goals
I'll go to the library. I won't go to the library.	go to the library / stay home / borrow some books / go on a picnic / visit one's uncle's house / eat out / read comic books / get a haircut / have a birthday party / have a barbecue / go to the movies / go to the concert / go shopping / stay up late	See you later. **Useful Questions** Will you come with us? What will you do?	• Talking about plans with "will" • Making affirmative/negative statements ● **Theme** Free time / Plans

REVIEW TEST 2   UNIT 05-08

WORD LIST

a dancer

a fashion designer

a lawyer

a pianist

a pilot

a reporter

an actor

an artist

a firefighter

a singer

a photographer

a movie director

an astronaut

an architect

UNIT 01

UNIT 01

UNIT 01

UNIT 01

UNIT 01

UNIT 01

UNIT 01

UNIT 01

UNIT 02

UNIT 01

UNIT 01

UNIT 01

UNIT 02

UNIT 01

UNIT 01

UNIT 01

a fever

a headache

a sore throat

get some rest

a cold

a toothache

a runny nose

lie down

a cough

take medicine

a backache

long hair

a stomachache

see a doctor

an earache

short hair

VOCABULARY FLASHCARDS

UNIT 03

UNIT 03

UNIT 03

UNIT 03

UNIT 02

UNIT 02

UNIT 02

UNIT 02

UNIT 02

UNIT 02

UNIT 02

UNIT 02

UNIT 02

UNIT 02

UNIT 02

UNIT 02
SCIENCE
FAIR

straight hair

a necklace

pigtails

the airport

curly hair

a headband

a mustache

the train station

a beard

blond hair

a ring

the subway
station

a tie

a ponytail

a bracelet

the
science fair

VOCABULARY FLASHCARDS

UNIT 03

UNIT 03

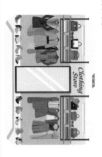

UNIT 03

POST OFFICE

UNIT 03

UNIT 04

UNIT 03

SUPER PRICE

UNIT 03

Clothing Store

UNIT 04

UNIT 04

UNIT 03

PET SHOP

UNIT 03

ZOO

UNIT 03

UNIT 04

UNIT 04

UNIT 03

TOYS

UNIT 03

the post office	the department store	the zoo	the swimming pool
the clothing store	the concert hall	the pet shop	the toy store
the aquarium	the supermarket	the sports center	funny
boring	exciting	disappointing	great

VOCABULARY FLASHCARDS

UNIT 05

UNIT 05

UNIT 05

UNIT 05

UNIT 04

UNIT 05

UNIT 05

UNIT 05

UNIT 04

UNIT 04

UNIT 04

UNIT 04

UNIT 04

UNIT 04

UNIT 04

UNIT 04

delicious	cheap	expensive	interesting
shocking	difficult	amazing	touching
scary	adventure stories	sci-fi stories	horror stories
comic books	action movies	comedies	classical music

UNIT 05

UNIT 05

UNIT 05

UNIT 05

UNIT 06

UNIT 05

UNIT 05

UNIT 06

UNIT 06

UNIT 06

UNIT 06

UNIT 06

UNIT 06

UNIT 06

UNIT 06

UNIT 06

hip-hop	dancing	jogging	camping
fishing	cycling	playing the guitar	a dancer
a fashion designer	a lawyer	a pianist	a pilot
a reporter	an actor	an artist	a firefighter

UNIT 07

UNIT 07

UNIT 06

UNIT 06

UNIT 07

UNIT 07

UNIT 07

UNIT 06

UNIT 07

UNIT 07

UNIT 07

UNIT 06

UNIT 07

UNIT 07

UNIT 07

UNIT 06

a singer

an architect

fly
an airplane

go hiking

a photographer

make a boat

blow bubbles

blow up
a balloon

a movie
director

make a kite

play with clay

climb
a rock wall

an astronaut

float a boat

take a trip

make origami

VOCABULARY FLASHCARDS

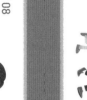

CINEMA

LIBRARY

Library

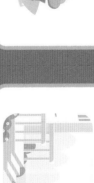

play with friends	stay home	eat out	have a barbecue
take a walk	borrow some books	read comic books	go to the movies
take a nap	go on a picnic	get a haircut	go to the concert
go to the library	visit one's uncle's house	have a birthday party	go shopping

stay up late

UNIT 01

I have

UNIT 02

He has

UNIT 02

He wears

UNIT 02

She has

UNIT 01

You should

UNIT 02

He doesn't have

UNIT 02

He doesn't wear

UNIT 02

She doesn't have

UNIT 02

She wears

UNIT 03

I'm going to

UNIT 04

It was

UNIT 05

I'm interested in

UNIT 02

She doesn't wear

UNIT 03

I'm not going to

UNIT 04

It wasn't

UNIT 05

I'm not interested in

UNIT 06

I want to be

UNIT 06

I don't want to be

UNIT 07

I'm going to

UNIT 07

I'm not going to

UNIT 08

I'll

UNIT 08

I won't

•

•

with 세이펜

원어민 음성을 실시간 반복학습	단어 및 대화의 우리말 해석 듣기	선생님의 Workbook Guide로 혼자서도 쉽게 학습

세이펜 핀파일 다운로드 안내

STEP 1 세이펜과 컴퓨터를 USB 케이블로 연결하세요.

STEP 2 쎄듀북 홈페이지(www.cedubook.com)에 접속 후, 학습자료실 메뉴에서 학습할 교재를 찾아 이동합니다.

> 초등교재 ▶ ELT ▶ 학습교재 클릭 ▶ 세이펜 핀파일 자료 클릭
> ▶ 다운로드 (저장을 '다른 이름으로 저장'으로 변경하여 저장소를 USB로 변경) ▶ 완료

STEP 3 음원 다운로드가 완료되면 세이펜과 컴퓨터의 USB 케이블을 분리하세요.

STEP 4 세이펜을 분리하면 "시스템을 초기화 중입니다. 잠시만 기다려 주세요." 라는 멘트가 나옵니다.

STEP 5 멘트 종료 후 세이펜을 〈Oh! My Speaking〉 표지에 대보세요.
효과음이 나온 후 바로 학습을 시작할 수 있습니다.

참고사항

◆ 세이펜은 본 교재에 포함되어 있지 않습니다. 별도로 구매하여 이용할 수 있으며, 기존에 보유하신 세이펜이 있다면 핀파일만 다운로드해서
바로 이용하실 수 있습니다.

◆ 세이펜에서 제작된 모든 기종(기존에 보유하고 계신 기종도 호환 가능)으로 사용이 가능합니다.

◆ 모든 기종은 세이펜에서 권장하는 최신 펌웨어 업데이트를 진행해 주시기 바랍니다.
업데이트는 세이펜 홈페이지(www.saypen.com)에서 가능합니다.

◆ 핀파일은 쎄듀북 홈페이지(www.cedubook.com)와 세이펜 홈페이지(www.saypen.com)에서 모두 다운로드 가능합니다.

◆ 세이펜을 이용하지 않는 학습자는 쎄듀북 홈페이지 부가학습자료, 교재 내 QR코드 이미지 등을 활용하여 원어민 음성으로 학습하실 수 있습니다.

◆ 기타 문의사항은 www.cedubook.com / 02-3272-4766으로 연락 바랍니다.

세이펜과 함께 배우는 Oh! My Speaking

〈Oh! My Speaking〉은 세이펜이 적용된 도서입니다. 세이펜을 가져다 대면 원어민의 생생한 영어 발음과 억양을 듣고 영어 말하기 연습을 할 수 있습니다.
*번역 기능 | 세이펜으로 책을 찍어서 원어민 음성을 들은 후, [T] 버튼을 짧게 누르면 우리말 해석 음원을 들을 수 있습니다.

✏️ 세이펜을 대면 유닛명을 들을 수 있습니다. [T] 기능 지원

✏️ QR코드에 세이펜을 대면 해당 MP3파일이 재생됩니다.

✏️ 세이펜을 대면 Activity의 지시문을 들을 수 있습니다. [T] 기능 지원

✏️ 그림이나 영어 단어에 세이펜을 대면 원어민의 발음을 들을 수 있습니다. [T] 기능 지원

✏️ 그림이나 말풍선에 세이펜을 대면 해당 문장을 들을 수 있습니다. [T] 기능 지원

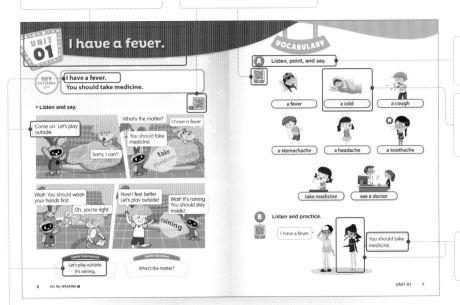

✏️ 영어 문장에 세이펜을 대면 원어민의 정확한 발음과 억양을 들을 수 있습니다. [T] 기능 지원

✏️ 번호에 세이펜을 대면 해당 그림에 대한 Key Pattern 대화가 재생되며, 그림이나 영어 단어에 세이펜을 대면 해당 영어 단어를 들을 수 있습니다. [T] 기능 지원

✏️ 영어 문장이나 단어에 세이펜을 대면 원어민의 정확한 발음과 억양을 들을 수 있습니다. [T] 기능 지원

✏️ 그림에 세이펜을 대면 해당 그림에 대한 Key Pattern 대화를 들을 수 있습니다. [T] 기능 지원

✏️ 문제 번호에 세이펜을 대면 해당 문제의 음원이 재생되며, 말풍선에 세이펜을 대면 해당 문장 또는 정답 영어 문장을 들을 수 있습니다. [T] 기능 지원

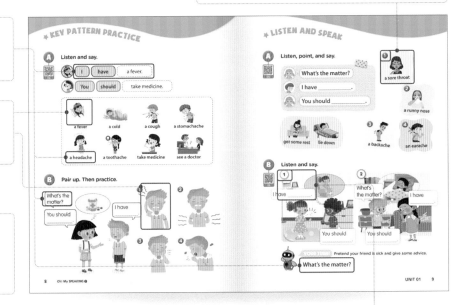

oh! my SPEAKING

5

Oh! My SPEAKING 5

WORKBOOK

CEDU BOOK

I have a fever.

A Look and write. Use the hints from the cue box.

HELP

1

2

3

4

5

6

Cue Box

stomachache	earache	fever
sore throat	toothache	backache

B What's the matter? Look and complete the sentences.

HELP

1

A: I have a c _____ .

B: You should t _____ m _____ .

2

A: I have a h _____ .

B: You should g _____ s _____ r _____ .

3

A: I have a r _____ n _____ .

B: You should s _____ a d _____ .

C Trace, unscramble, and write.

1

 What's the matter?

 _____

a / I / cough / have / .

2

 _____

toothache / have / a / I /.

 _____

should / You / a / see / doctor / .

3

 What's the matter?

 _____

sore throat / I / a / have / .

4

 What's the matter?

 _____

have / backache / a / I / .

 _____

lie down / should / You / .

D Listen and write O if the dialogue and the picture match, and X if they don't.

1

2

3

4

E Listen and choose the right sentence for the blank.

1

ⓐ ⓑ ⓒ

What's the matter?

_____.

2

ⓐ ⓑ ⓒ

I have a runny nose.

_____.

F Put the dialogue in the correct order.
Then listen to it and practice with a friend.

Wacky: Come on. Let's play outside.

Jack: Sorry, I can't.

Wacky: You should take medicine.

Jack: I have a fever.

Wacky: What's the matter?

Jack: Now I feel better.

YOUR TURN! What's the matter?
Give them some advice.

A: I have a _____ .
B: You should _____ .

A: I have a _____ .
B: You should _____ .

Advice

He has long hair.

A Write and find the words.

HELP

1

4

2

5

3

6

n	z	a	b	e	a	r	d	z	p
t	e	o	s	f	c	l	n	b	o
n	t	c	a	q	u	t	s	j	n
k	t	s	k	b	n	z	a	s	y
s	i	a	k	l	g	c	d	a	t
t	e	d	r	z	a	k	e	d	a
k	y	s	t	j	d	c	t	s	i
m	u	s	t	a	c	h	e	a	l
e	q	s	t	a	o	r	g	k	d
w	c	b	r	a	c	e	l	e	t

B Look and complete the sentences.

HELP

1

He has b _____ h _____.

He has a b _____.

2

She has c _____ h _____.

She wears a t _____.

3

He has l _____ h _____.

He wears a n _____.

C Trace, unscramble, and write.

1

_____
a / has / She / ponytail / .

_____
wears / necklace / She / a / .

2

_____
straight hair / He / has / .

_____
He / tie / wears / a / .

3  Does she have long hair?

 No. _____
doesn't / long hair / She / have / .

_____
short hair / She / has / .

4  Does he wear a bracelet?

 No. _____
bracelet / doesn't / a / wear / He / .

_____
wears / He / a / ring / .

D Listen and write O if the dialogue and the picture match, and X if they don't.

HELP

1

2

3

4

E Listen and choose the right sentence for the blank.

HELP

1

 Does she wear a ring?

 _____.

2

 Does he have long hair?

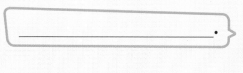 _____.

F **Put the dialogue in the correct order.**
Then listen to it and practice with a friend.

Wacky: Does he have a beard?

Jack: Yes. He wears big glasses.

Jack: No. He doesn't have a beard.

Wacky: Does he wear glasses?

Jack: There he is!

Wacky: Hi, Uncle Joe!

 **YOUR TURN!** Describe your friend's appearance and accessories.

He/She has _____ , but

he/she doesn't have _____ .

He/She wears _____ , but

he/she doesn't wear _____ .

I'm going to the airport.

A

Fill in the blanks below each picture to complete the word.

1

_ _ _ ari _ m

2

_ _ u _ er
_ _ r _ et

3

_ e _ _ _ op

4

_ _ part _ en _
s _ _ re

5

p _ _ _ _
o _ _ i _ _ _

6

_ on _ _ _ t
_ a _ _ _

B

Look and complete the sentences.

1

A: Where are you going?

B: I'm going to the s_____ s_____.

2

A: Are you going to the zoo?

B: Yes. I'm going to the z_____.

3

A: Are you going to the train station?

B: No. I'm not going to the t_____ s_____.

I'm going to the a_____.

Trace, unscramble, and write.

1 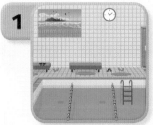 Where are you going?

_____

going to / I'm / swimming pool / the / .

2  Where are you going?

_____

I'm / the / going to / toy store / .

3  Are you going to the sports

center?

 Yes.
_____

going to / the / I'm / sports center / .

4  Are you going to the aquarium?

 No.
_____

I'm / aquarium / not / the / going to / .

_____

science fair / I'm / the / going to / .

Where are you going? Listen and number.

Where are you going?

Are you going to
_____?

E **Listen and choose the right sentence for the blank.**

1

Are you going to
the swimming pool?

_____ .

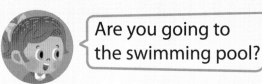

a   b   c

2

Where are you going?

_____ .

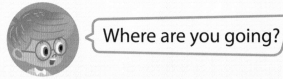

a   b   c

F Put the dialogue in the correct order.
Then listen to it and practice with a friend.

85
HELP

Jack: Where are you going?

Wacky: I'm going to the airport. ▢

Amy: No. I'm not going to the airport. ▢

Wacky: Are you going to the airport, too? ▢

Amy: I'm going to the train station. I'm going to my grandmother's house in Busan.

Wacky: Lucky!

 **YOUR TURN!** Where are you going? Choose and complete the sentences.

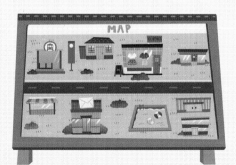

A: Where are you going?

B: I'm going to the _____ .
　　　　　　　　　　(place)

A: Where's the _____ ?
　　　　　　　　　(place)

B: It's _____ .
　　　　　(location)

UNIT 04 — It was funny.

A Unscramble and write the words.

(HELP)

1

p c e a h

_____

2

h i s o c n g k

_____

3

n y n f u

_____

4

c u s i e l i o d

_____

5

a r s c y

_____

6

f i u l d i f c t

_____

B Look and complete the sentences.

(HELP)

1

A: How was the movie?

B: It was t _____.

2

A: Was it boring?

B: Yes. It was b _____.

3

A: Was it expensive?

B: No. It wasn't e _____.

It was c _____.

C Trace, unscramble, and write.

1  How was the movie?

_____
was / It / interesting / .

2 Was it amazing?

Yes. _____
It / amazing / was / .

3 Was it difficult?

Yes. _____
difficult / It / was / .

4 Was it disappointing?

No. _____
It / disappointing / wasn't / .

_____
was / It / great / .

D Listen and write O if the dialogue and the picture match, and X if they don't.

1

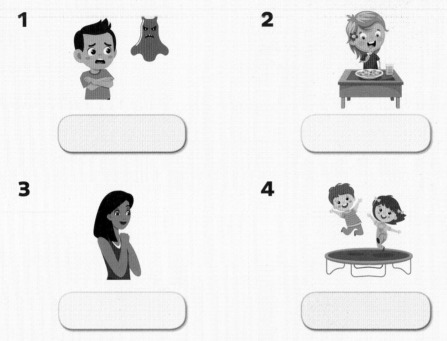

2

3

4

E Listen and choose the right sentence for the blank.

1

How was the movie?

a b c _____.

2

Was it boring?

a b c _____.

F Put the dialogue in the correct order.
Then listen to it and practice with a friend.

Mom: How was the movie?

Jack: It was funny and exciting!

Wacky: It wasn't funny. It was boring.

Wacky: Yes. It was too long.

Mom: Was it too long?

Jack: But the popcorn was delicious.

Wacky: Oh my!

YOUR TURN! How was the movie? Complete the sentences below.

A: How was the movie?

B: It was _____.

A: Was it _____?

B: Yes. It was _____.

UNIT 05

I'm interested in adventure stories.

A Look and write. Use the hints from the cue box.

1

_____

2

_____

3

_____

4

_____

5

_____

6

_____

> **Cue Box** fishing   camping   action movies
>   comedies   sci-fi stories   jogging

B Look and complete the sentences.

1

A: What kind of books do you like?

B: I'm interested in c_____ b_____.

2

A: Are you interested in classical music?

B: Yes. I'm interested in c_____ m_____.

3

A: Are you interested in dancing?

B: No. I'm not interested in d_____.

I'm interested in p_____ the guitar.

C **Trace, unscramble, and write.**

HELP

1

 What kind of books do you like?

 _____

interested in / adventure stories / I'm / .

2

 Are you interested in hip-hop?

 Yes. _____

I'm / hip-hop / interested in / .

3

 Are you interested in action

movies? _____

 Yes. _____

interested in / I'm / action movies / .

4

 Are you interested in horror

stories? _____

 No. _____

interested in / not / horror stories / I'm / .

_____

I'm / sci-fi stories / interested in / .

D Listen and see what the child is interested in.
Draw O under the picture if the child is interested in it and
X if not.

E Listen and choose the right sentence for the blank.

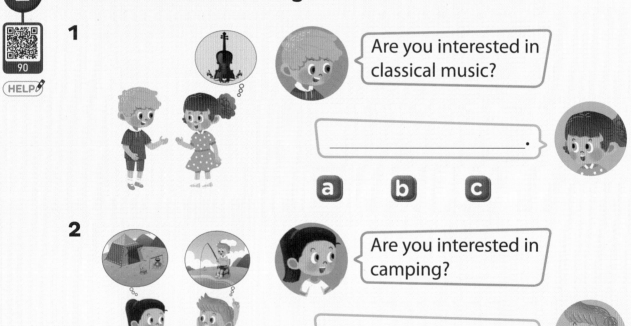

F Put the dialogue in the correct order.
Then listen to it and practice with a friend.

Amy: Are you interested in sci-fi stories?

Wacky: Yes. I'm interested in sci-fi stories. ☐

Jack: No. I'm not interested in horror stories. ☐

Amy: How about horror stories? ☐

Amy: You really enjoy reading books!

Jack & Wacky: Yes, we do.

 What are you interested in?
Complete the sentences below.

I'm interested in _____ .

I'm not interested in _____ .

UNIT 06 I want to be a scientist.

A Write and find the words.

(HELP)

1

4

2

5

3

6

b	a	z	a	p	i	l	o	t	x
d	t	s	o	b	i	u	r	j	i
a	x	t	a	q	z	t	s	p	p
k	w	a	s	r	b	k	z	v	i
s	y	c	a	k	o	g	c	d	a
i	g	t	d	r	a	n	k	e	n
n	k	o	a	x	l	e	a	q	i
g	q	r	t	n	j	t	g	u	s
e	n	z	w	q	s	z	k	e	t
r	e	p	o	r	t	e	r	y	r

B Look and complete the sentences.

(HELP)

1

A: What do you want to be?

B: I want to be an a_____.

2

A: Do you want to be a dancer?

B: Yes. I want to be a d_____.

3

A: Do you want to be a photographer?

B: No. I don't want to be a p_____.

I want to be a l_____.

C Trace, unscramble, and write.

HELP✎

1

What do you want to be?

_____

I / fashion designer / to be / want / a / .

2

Do you want to be a firefighter?

Yes. _____

to be / a / want / I / firefighter / .

3

What do you want to be?

_____

I / to be / movie director / a / want / .

4

Do you want to be an artist?

No. _____

want / I / don't / to be / artist /an / .

_____

architect / want / to be / an / I / .

D What do you want to be? Listen and number.

92
HELP

E Listen and choose the right sentence for the blank.

93
HELP

1

What do you want to be?

_____.

a   b   c

2

Do you want to be a fashion designer?

_____.

a   b   c

F Put the dialogue in the correct order.
Then listen to it and practice with a friend.

Mom: What do you want to be?

Mom: Amy, do you want to be a scientist, too?

Jack: I want to be a scientist… like you.

Amy: No. I don't want to be a scientist.
I want to be a teacher.

Amy: Jack, sit down. Open your book.

Jack: No. I don't want to study now.

YOUR TURN! What do you want to be? Look and complete the sentences.

I don't want to be a(an) _____,

but I want to be a(an) _____.

I'm going to make a boat.

A Fill in the blanks below each picture to complete the word.

(HELP)

1

__ __ o w
__ u b b __ __ s

2

__ a __ e
o __ __ g a __ __

3

__ __ __
h __ __ __ n g

4
__ __ k e
a __ i __ __ __

5

__ a k __
a __ __ l __

6

p __ __ y with
__ __ i e __ __ s

B Look and complete the sentences.

1

A: What are you going to do?
B: I'm going to m _____ a boat.

2

A: Are you going to take a trip?
B: Yes. I'm going to t _____ a trip.

3

A: Are you going to take a nap?
B: No. I'm not going to t _____ a nap.
I'm going to c _____ a rock wall.

C Trace, unscramble, and write.

1

 What are you going to do?

 _____

float a boat / I'm / going to / .

2

 Are you going to play with clay?

 Yes. _____

I'm / play with clay / going to / .

3

 What are you going to do?

 _____

going to / take a walk / I'm / .

4

 Are you going to blow up a balloon?

 No. _____

blow up a balloon / going to / I'm / not / .

_____

going to / I'm / fly an airplane / .

HELP

D What are you going to do? Listen and number.

HELP

E Listen and choose the right sentence for the blank.

1

What are you going to do?

_____.

 a   b   c

2

Are you going to take a walk?

_____.

 a   b c

F Put the dialogue in the correct order.
Then listen to it and practice with a friend.

Wacky: What are you going to do with the chopsticks?

Wacky: No. I'm not going to make a boat.
I'm going to make a kite.

Jack: I'm going to make a boat.

Jack: Are you going to make a boat, too?

Jack: Good idea!

YOUR TURN! Choose the activities and write what you are and aren't going to do.

A: What are you going to do?

Are you going to _____ ?

B: Yes. I _____ , but I _____ .

I'll go to the library.

A Unscramble and write the words.

1

_____ out

2

go _____

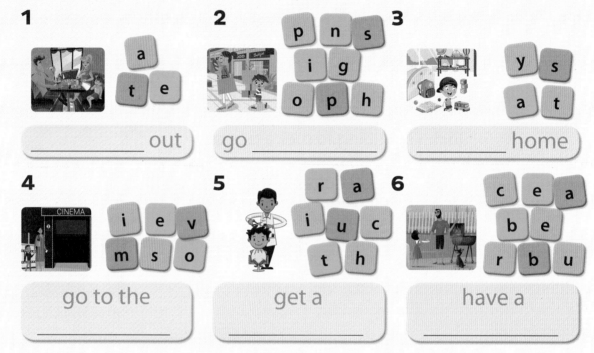

3

_____ home

4

go to the

_____

5

get a

_____

6

have a

_____

B Look and complete the sentences.

1

A: What will you do?

B: I'll r_____ comic books.

2

A: Will you borrow some books?

B: Yes. I'll b_____ some books.

3

A: Will you go on a picnic?

B: No. I won't g_____ on a picnic.

I'll v_____ my uncle's house.

Trace, unscramble, and write.

1

What will you do?

_____

my uncle's house / I'll / visit / .

2

Will you go to the library?

Yes. _____

I'll / to the library / go / .

3

What will you do?

_____

have / a birthday party / I'll / .

4

Will you go shopping?

No. _____

I / go shopping / won't / .

_____

to the movies / go / I'll / .

D What will you do? Listen and number.

E Listen and choose the right sentence for the blank.

1

What will you do?

_____.

2

Will you go to the concert?

_____.

F

Put the dialogue in the correct order.
Then listen to it and practice with a friend.

Mom: I'll go to the library.

Jack: I'll go with you.

Mom: Okay. Wacky, will you come with us?

Mom: What will you do?

Wacky: No. I won't go to the library.
I'll just stay home.

Wacky: I'll play a computer game, but I won't play too much.

Choose the activities.
Write and talk about what you'll do this weekend.

A: What will you do this weekend?

B: I'll _____, but I won't _____.

WORKBOOK GUIDE

- Try to do the workbook activities on your own as much as possible.
- If you need additional help or want to hear the answers, scan the appropriate QR code below using your phone.
- You will be able to listen to the teacher's explanation immediately!

UNIT 01

A   B   C   D   E   F

UNIT 02

A   B   C   D   E   F

UNIT 03

A   B   C   D   E   F

UNIT 04

A   B   C   D   E   F

UNIT 05

 A   B   C   D   E   F

UNIT 06

 A   B C   D   E   F

UNIT 07

A B   C   D   E   F

UNIT 08

 A   B   C   D   E   F

Oh! My Speaking is a six-level speaking series designed for young learners. With task-based activities and vivid illustrations, *Oh! My Speaking* allows students to build up their confidence in speaking and to communicate with their peers in fun and interesting ways. By focusing on basic key words and key patterns with *Oh! My Speaking*, students set out on the journey toward becoming strong speakers of English.

Oh! My Speaking Series

Oh! My Speaking
SD4-OHMS

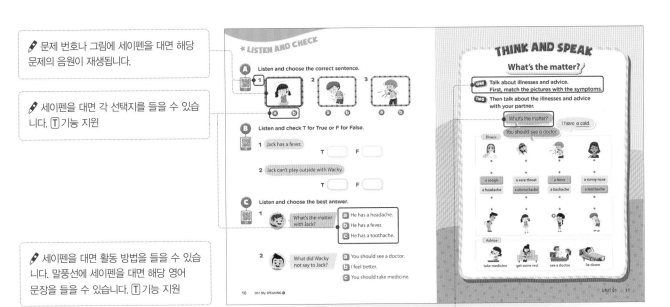

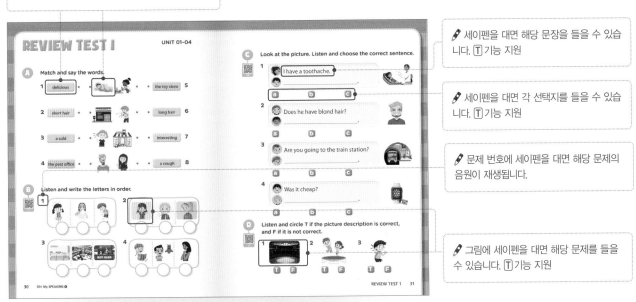

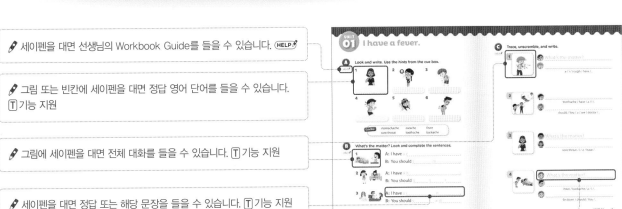

초등코치 천일문과
세이펜의 만남!

초등코치 천일문 시리즈 ✕ 세이펜 학습의 장점

01	02	03	04	05
녹음기능을 활용하여 발음 교정 및 쉐도잉 학습 가능	112개 대표 패턴 및 모든 문장을 원어민 발음으로 실시간 재생	게임모드를 활용한 즐거운 영어학습 가능	Role play를 이용한 가상 대화 체험 (Sentence에 한함)	이해하기 어려운 문법적 내용을 쉬운 해설과 함께 바로듣기 가능 (Grammar에 한함)

* 〈초등코치 천일문 시리즈〉는 세이펜이 적용된 도서입니다.
  세이펜을 영어에 가져다 대기만 하면 원어민이 들려주는 생생한 영어 발음과 억양을 바로 확인할 수 있습니다.

* 세이펜은 본 교재에 포함되어 있지 않습니다. 기존에 보유하신 세이펜이 있다면 핀파일만 다운로드해서 바로 이용하실 수 있습니다.
  단, Role-Play 기능은 SBS-1000 이후 모델에서만 구동됩니다.